UPRIGHTNESS BETRAYED:

The Assassination of Thomas Sankara of Burkina Faso and the Suffocation of Hope in Africa

Janvier T. Chando

TISI BOOKS

NEW YORK, RALEIGH, LONDON, AMSTERDAM

Non-Fiction Titles by Janvier T. Chando

HEGEMON IN THE MAKING: THE BIRTH AND GROWTH…
FALLEN HEROES: African Leaders Whose Assassinations…
ICONS AND VILLAINS: Recent Political Assassinations…
UKRAINE: The Tug-of-War Between Russia and the West
CAMEROON: The Haunted Heart of Africa

Fiction Titles by Janvier Chando

The Usurper: and Other Stories
Triple Agent, Double Cross
Disciples of Fortune
The Union Moujik
Flash of the Sun
Good Fortune Calls
Master of Good Fortune
Good Fortune's Children
The Girl on the Trail
Me Before Them
The Grandmothers and Perfect Love
The Fire and Ice Legend
The Sweetest Madness
The Hunger Fire
The Shades of Fire
Father and Sons
Fateful Ties
The Verdict of Hades
His Majesty's Trial
Ngoko's Folly
The Usurper
The Dowry
I am Hated
The Oaf

Upcoming Titles by Janvier Chando

The Home Drifters
The Mortal Friends
The White Hawk
The Norilsk Bears

Acknowledgement

Special words of appreciation to Franklyn Bayen, Salomon Muna T. Yakana, Eric Nkabyo, Idris Doh, Julius Wakam, Sampson Baiyc, Gabriel Nkeng, Linus Chinda, Wilson Okole, Rodney Musoko and Valentine Forchak with whom we discussed the Sankara legacy and arrived at insightful conclusions.

Dedication

The book is dedicated to all iconic and legendary leaders whose purposes were to serve humanity and advance the wellbeing of mankind, especially those who were cut short in their historic missions by the evil forces of this world.

UPRIGHTNESS BETRAYED:

The Assassination of Thomas Sankara of Burkina Faso and the Suffocation of Hope in Africa

UPRIGHTNESS BETRAYED:

The Assassination of Thomas Sankara of Burkina Faso
and the Suffocation of Hope in Africa

Quotes by Thomas Sankara

"While revolutionaries as individuals can be murdered, you cannot kill ideas."

"The enemy is not the one who is facing you with a sword in hand, that's the opponent. The enemy is the one behind you with a knife at your back."

"Without patriotic political education, a soldier is only a potential criminal."

"I do not think that Blaise (Blaise Compaoré, his deputy and best friend) wants to make an attempt on my life. The only danger is that if he refuses to act, the imperialist powers will offer him power on a silver platter by organizing my assassination. Even if they succeed in assassinating me, it does not matter! The bottom line is that they want to eat, and I am stopping them. But I shall die peacefully, for never, after what we have succeeded in instilling in the consciences of our countrymen, they cannot control our people as formerly."

"The greatest difficulty we have faced is the neocolonial way of thinking that exists in this country. We were colonized by a country, France, that left us with certain habits. For us, being successful in life, being happy, meant trying to live as they do in France, like the richest of the French."

"You cannot carry out fundamental change without a certain amount of madness. In this case, it comes from nonconformity, the courage to turn your back on the old formulas, the courage to invent the future."

"Debt is a cleverly managed reconquest of Africa. It is a reconquest that turns each one of us into a financial slave."

"Let there be an end to the arrogance of the big powers who miss no opportunity to put the rights of the people in question. Africa's absence from the club of those who have the right to veto is unjust and should be ended."

"We are not against progress, but we do not want progress that is anarchic and criminally neglects the rights of others."

"Inequality can be done away with only by establishing a new society, where men and women will enjoy equal rights…Thus, the status of women will improve only with the elimination of the system that exploits them."

"The spirit is smothered, as it were, by ignorance, but as soon as ignorance is destroyed, the spirit shines forth like the sun when it breaks through clouds."

"The patriarchal family made its appearance, founded on the sole and personal property of the father, who had become head of the family. Within this family, the woman was oppressed."

"I want people to remember me as someone whose life has been helpful to humanity."

"Our country produces enough to feed us all. Alas, for lack of organization, we are forced to beg for food aid. It's this aid that instills in our spirits the attitude of beggars."

"Everything that man can imagine, he is capable of creating."

"It took the madmen of yesterday for us to be able to act with extreme clarity today. I want to be one of those madmen. We must dare to invent the future."

"If you take a walk around Ouagadougou and make a list of the mansions you see, you will note that they belong to just a minority. How many of you who have been assigned to Ouagadougou from the farthest corners of the country have had to move every night because you've been thrown out of the house you have rented? To those who have acquired houses and land through corruption, we say: start to tremble. If you have stolen, tremble, because we will come after you."

"We must dare to invent the future."

"Women hold up the other half of the sky."

"We make every effort to see that our actions live up to our words and be vigilant with regards to our behavior."

"Comrades, there is no true social revolution without the liberation of women."

"It's really a pity that there are observers who view political events like comic strips. There has to be a Zorro, there has to be a star. No, the problem of Upper Volta is more serious than that. It was a grave mistake to have looked for a man, a star, at all costs, to the point of creating one, that is, to the point of attributing the ownership of the event to captain Sankara, who must have been the brains, etc."

"Our revolution in Burkina Faso draws on the totality of man's experiences since the first breath of humanity. We wish to be the heirs of all the revolutions of the world, of all the liberation struggles of the peoples of the Third World. We draw the lessons of the American revolution."

"The Revolution Cannot Triumph Without the Emancipation of Women."

"The revolution and women's liberation go together. We do not talk of women's emancipation as an act of charity or out of a surge of human compassion. It is a basic necessity for the revolution to triumph. Women hold up the other half of the sky."

"Imperialism is a system of exploitation that occurs not only in the brutal form of those who come with guns to conquer territory. Imperialism often occurs in more subtle forms, a loan, food aid, blackmail. We are fighting this system that allows a handful of men on earth to rule all of humanity."

"We have to work at decolonizing our mentality and achieving happiness within the limits of sacrifice we should be willing to make. We have to recondition our people to accept themselves as they are, to not be ashamed of their real situation, to be satisfied with it, to glory in it, even."

"The enemies of a people are those who keep them in ignorance."

"The French revolution taught us the rights of man."

"Comrades, there is no true social revolution without the liberation of women. May my eyes never see, and my fcct never take me to a society where half the people are held in silence. I hear the roar of women's silence. I sense the rumble of their storm and feel the fury of their revolt."

"We must learn to live the African way. It's the only way to live in freedom and with dignity."

"He who feeds you, controls you."

"Under its current form, that is imperialism-controlled, debt is a cleverly managed re-conquest of Africa, aiming at subjugating its growth and development through foreign rules. Thus, each one of us becomes the financial slave, which is to say a true slave."

"May my eyes never see, and my feet never take me to a society where half the people are held in silence."

"He who does not feed you can demand nothing of you."

"Inequality can be done away with only by establishing a new society, where men and women will enjoy equal rights, resulting from an upheaval in the means of production and in all social relations. Thus, the status of women will improve only with the elimination of the system that exploits them."

"Che Guevara taught us we could dare to have confidence in ourselves, confidence in our abilities. He instilled in us the conviction that struggle is our only recourse. He was a citizen of the free world that together we are in the process of building. That is why we say that Che Guevara is also African and Burkinabè."

"Never be ashamed of being Afrikan."

"When the people stand up, imperialism trembles."

Contents

MAPS

Burkina Faso on a map of the world

Burkina Faso on a Map of Africa

Partition map of Africa (1884-1914)

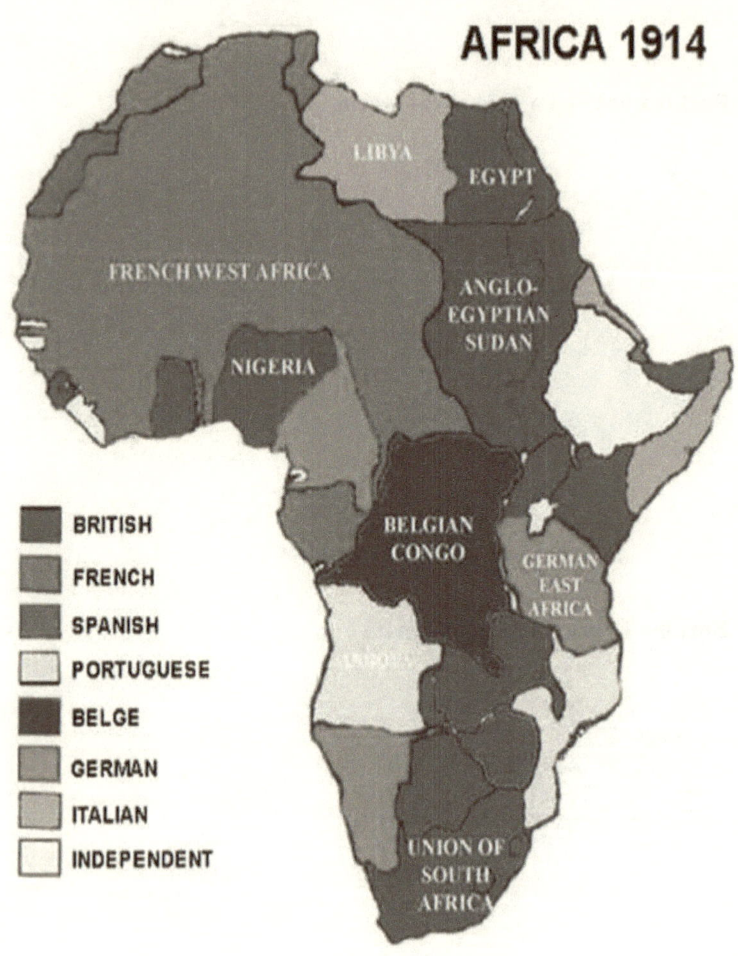

INTRODUCTION

In my search for the answer to why certain geopolitical flashpoints exist in the world, in my pry to know the reason(s) why some countries and the world in general experienced sudden and dramatic changes that led to war, instability or a reorientation of their domestic and foreign policies that not only affected these countries but also influence certain regions or the whole world, I explored political assassinations over the past dozens of decades that changed our world. By our world, I mean our communities, countries, regions, and humanity as a whole.

In treating the different assassinations that took place over the years, I used an approach characterized by political sociology, where I succinctly analyzed the historical and social factors that not only led to the assassinations, but that also arose from the killing of these historical figures. And from these factors, we are presented with an idea or pictures of how the society affected has evolved since the traumatic event(s).

From the backlashes that followed the assassination of historic, legendary, or iconic figures, we can learn something useful and come up with scenarios or what to expect as calamities if particular leaders are assassinated, and so act accordingly in preventing their assassinations.

Chapter One

Thomas Sankara

When Africa woke up that morning of October 16, 1987, and learned of the death of Thomas Sankara, the charismatic head of state of Burkina Faso, shock, grief, and melancholy settled over the continent. When more news sipped in reporting that he was killed along with twelve others in a military coup d'état led by the then Vice President Blaise Compaoré, (who after the coup became the president and ruled until his ouster in a popular uprising on October 31, 2014), the Burkina Faso masses were outraged. Thomas Sankara had made known to the world that Blaise Compaoré was his chum and closest confidant.

So, who was this young man who took a landlocked country in Africa out of an impasse, a territory that was the heartland of the Songhai Empire, and then showed the people there and their brethren in the rest of Africa the path to a future devoid of the retarding influence of neocolonialism?

Chapter Two

The story begins in 1949, with the birth of Thomas Sankara on December 21 of that year in Yako, Upper Volta, and became legendary with his death on Oct 15, 1987, in Ouagadougou, Burkina Faso from the bullets of his assassins. However, we shall deal with the chapters that constitute his life on earth as we delve deeper into how he became the leader of the Burkinabe Revolution before his untimely death.

Sankara's rise to the highest office of the land began following his training as a pilot and after he became a captain in the Upper Volta Air Force. But it wasn't only his skills as a pilot that made him a popular figure in the country's capital city called Ouagadougou, especially after fighting in the 1974 border war against Mali. The fact that he was a decent guitarist and the fact that he liked motorbikes may also have contributed to his charisma. So, his appointment as Secretary of State for Information in 1981 by Colonel Saye Zerbo, who became the president of the country after ending the 14-year rule of Sangoulé Lamizana with a coup d'état on 25 November 1980, was welcomed by the country folks. However, when Sankara resigned from the government on 21 April 1982, citing the regime's anti-labor drift, the population saw another laudable side of his character that was uncommon around. He was incorruptible.

The November 07, 1982, coup d'état led by Major Doctor Jean-Baptiste Ouédraogo and the Council of Popular Salvation (CSP) that overthrew Colonel Saye Zerbo brought about the resuscitation of Sankara's fortunes when the new president made him Prime minister in 1983. But then, Jean-Christophe Mitterrand, the son of French President Francois Mitterrand who happened to be his father's African Affairs adviser, visited Upper Volta that year, did not like the young Sankara's political ideas, bluntness, and incorruptible nature, and so made the Upper Voltan president place Sankara and some of his close associates under house arrest. His confinement by the authorities triggered a popular uprising that could not be contained.

The Sankara saga would not have taken new dimensions had a group of men in Upper Volta, known today as Burkina Faso, not decided to launch a revolution that would enable the country "to accept the responsibility of its reality and its destiny with human dignity". A coup d'état organized by Blaise Compaoré with the help of Captain

Henri Bongo, Major Jean-Baptiste Booker Lingam, and the charismatic Captain Thomas Sankara deposed Jean-Baptiste Ouedraogo on 4 August 1983, after which they pronounced Thomas Sankara the leader. The 33-year-old Sankara went on to become a prominent figure in the group of African leaders who wanted to give the continent in general, and their countries in particular, a new socio-political dimension devoid of the shackles of neocolonialism, especially the overbearing French control of its former African colonies and territories.

Colonization of Africa and Dates of Independence

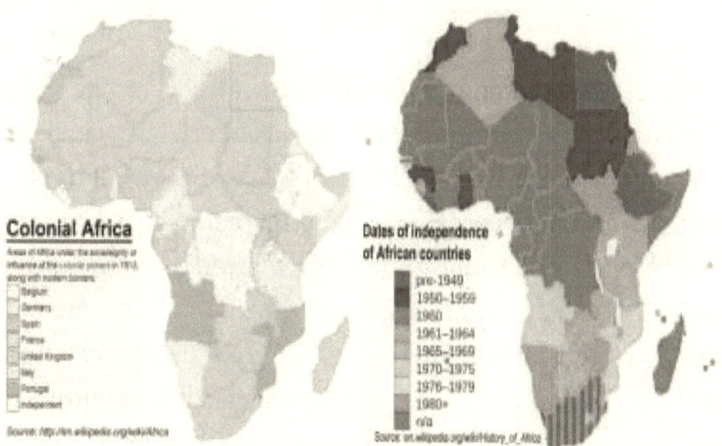

Thomas Sankara, the charismatic left-leaning leader of a country in the heart of West Africa was sometimes nicknamed "Tom Sank" and was considered by some of his admirers as an "African Che Guevara" even before he became the head of state of the country following the coup masterminded by his friend Blaise Compaoré.

Chapter Three

A year after assuming the highest office in the land, Sankara began the most ambitious programs for social and economic change ever attempted in any of the countries on the African continent. He changed the name of the country from Upper Volta to Burkina Faso, meaning "the land of upright people" in Mossi and Dyula, which are the country's two major languages. He also came up with a new flag and a new anthem for the enthusiastic country.

The young president would orient the country's policy towards fighting corruption, reforestation, averting famine, and towards making education and healthcare real priorities for the nation.

His domestic policies focused on:

- preventing famine with agrarian self-sufficiency and land reform that resulted in food self-sufficiency three years into his presidency

- making education a priority, which the government was relentless in pursuing through a nationwide literacy campaign
- and promoting public health by vaccinating 2, 500, 000 (2.5 million) children against meningitis, yellow fever, and measles.

Other laudable aspects of his national agenda included:

- the planting of over 10, 000, 000 (ten million) trees, which went a long way in halting the growing desertification of the Sahel
- the doubling of wheat production by redistributing land from feudal landlords to peasants
- the suspension of rural poll taxes and domestic rents
- and the launch of an ambitious road and railway construction program to "tie the nation together".

At the local level, Sankara also led the drive for every village to build a medical dispensary, and for over 350 communities to build schools using their own labor.

Right after he came to power, he became the champion of women's emancipation and rights in Africa. In fact, this was confirmed by his ban on female genital mutilation; his abolition of forced marriages, child marriages and polygamy; as well as by his policies and efforts encouraging women to take up leadership positions in the government and society, especially by appointing women to high governmental positions, and encouraging them to work outside the home and to stay in school, even if they became pregnant. When he wrote that:

"The revolution and women's liberation go together. We do not talk of women's emancipation as an act of charity or because of a surge of human compassion. It is a basic necessity for the triumph of the revolution. Women hold up the other half of the sky."

It was a reflection of his determination to improve the wellbeing of women in his country and Africa.

Sankara and Fidel Castro of Cuba

Chapter Four

Sankara pursued a foreign policy that did not condone imperialism and that encouraged cooperation based on respect and the recognition of Burkina Faso's interests as well as the interest of the other parties dealing with Burkina Faso. This saw his government eschewing all foreign aid, pushing for debt reduction in an audacious manner, and nationalizing all land and mineral wealth, thereby averting the power and influence of the International Monetary Fund (IMF) and its sister financial institution the World Bank.

Being one of the poorest countries in the world at the time, Burkina Faso was expected to continue kowtowing to its former colonial master and the international financial institutions. But Sankara was different. He was firmly convinced that the country could come around and sustain itself without foreign aid. He even went as far as refusing aid packages from the International Monetary Fund, which it gave with conditions attached to them that compromised Burkina Faso's sovereignty, as he saw it. He articulated this independence stance through numerous writings, speeches, interviews, and other exchanges. But at a period just after the independence of the 1960s when most of the continent's revolutionary, pan-Africanist and daring leaders had been killed, overthrown, and cowed or humbled by threats, sanctions, sabotage, and other active measures; Sankara came across as a voice that was not being heeded. He thought he found a forum to sell his crusade at the July 1987 summit of the Organization of African Unity, where he tried to persuade the heads of state of other African countries to act collectively and not pay their financial debts to their former colonizers, pointing out that:

> *"The origins of debt go back to colonialism's origins...We cannot repay the debt because we are not responsible for this debt. On the contrary, others owe us something that no money can pay for. That is to say, the debt of blood..."*

Even though Sankara's revolutionary programs for self-reliance transformed him into an icon in the eyes of many of Africa's poor and increased his popularity with most of the impoverished citizens of Burkina Faso, his policies undermined the vested interests of a wide range of groups (the Francophile Burkinabe middle-class, the tribal leaders who resented the fact that he stripped them of their long-held traditional privileges to forced labor and payment of tributes, and France and its ally the Ivory Coast under Félix Houphouet-Boigny, whom he considered a puppet of France). So, when Blaise Compaoré orchestrated his overthrow and assassination on 15 October 1987, many people (Burkinabes and non-Burkinabes) were left wondering whether he did not see it coming. After all, a week before his assassination, he had declared that:

> *"While revolutionaries as individuals can be murdered, you cannot kill ideas."*

His intuition was at play all right, but he did not seem to be the type that was prepared to go through the horrors of investigating and eliminating those he had been working closely with. He, like many great figures in history, understood that betrayal from those close to you is not your fault, especially if you, as the leader, never harbored evil intentions against your associates or comrades. In fact, he had a speech with him on the morning of his death that he had prepared the night before aimed at bridging the ideological rifts that were growing between the feuding factions in his government. An excerpt of it reads thus: *"Whatever the contradictions, whatever the oppositions, solutions will be found as long as confidence reigns..."* But he did not get to read that speech in the council meeting that morning because machine gun shots interrupted the proceedings just before it started, followed by shouts ordering everyone out. He let his fear-stricken ministers know that he was the one the gunmen were after, ordered them to stay put, raised his hands in the air, and then walked out to find his bodyguards lying dead on the stairs. Just then, the squad of attacking soldiers opened fire on him.

When the news of Thomas Sankara's assassination on October 15, 1987, went out shortly after he and twelve other officials were killed in a coup d'état organized by his former colleague Blaise Compaoré, it was received with outrage, sadness, apprehension, and disbelief in all of the countries of the world. But nowhere was the grief as great as in Burkina Faso and the rest of Africa where he was regarded by the masses as the beacon of hope in a continent dominated by leaders with the evil disposition, most of whom were puppets of foreign powers. Blaise Compaoré not only made sure Sankara got buried in an unmarked grave, but he also desecrated Sankara's legacy even further by reversing most of his policies and by realigning Burkina Faso with those foreign leaders and countries that were hostile to Sankara, especially the former colonial master France. Many people versed with history wasted no time in comparing Blaise Compaoré to Brutus (Marcus Julius Brutus), a politician of the Roman Republic who participated in the assassination of his close friend, the Roman Emperor Julius Caesar.

The fact that Blaise Compare would have Henri Zongo and Jean-Baptiste Boukary Lingani, whom he had initially been ruling in a triumvirate, arrested, charged with plotting to overthrow the government; the fact that the arrested were summarily tried, condemned, and then executed in September 1989, proves that Sankara was a trusting and trusted member in that group that seized power in 1983 and began the Burkinabe Revolution.

Sankara's quest to realize the most ambitious programs for social and economic change ever attempted on the African continent ended up as a partially realized dream, but it was a vision that is appreciated for stirring the hopes of the African youth. Today, he is a legend in his country and Africa three decades after his death.

Antonio de Figueiredo, a journalist, activist, and broadcaster who campaigned for the liberation of Portugal's African colonies, and who did more than anyone to bring the issue of colonial oppression in Angola, Mozambique, Guinea, and Cape Verde to the attention of the English-speaking world, understood the magnitude of Thomas Sankara's influence when he wrote in February 2008 that:

> *"Africa and the world are yet to recover from Sankara's assassination. Just as we have yet to recover from the loss of Patrice Lumumba, Kwame Nkrumah, Eduardo Mondlane, Amilcar Cabral, Steve Biko, Samora Machel, and most recently John Garang, to name only a few. While malevolent forces have not used the same methods to eliminate each of these great pan-Africanists, they have been guided by the same motive: to keep Africa in chains."*

Thomas Sankara, the revolutionary and short-lived head of state of Burkina Faso who reduced his salary to 450 US Dollars, sold the government's fleet of Mercedes Benz cars, banned the allocation of chauffeurs for government officials and made the Renault 5 the official car, was commemorated in ceremonies that took place in Burkina Faso, Mali, Senegal, Niger, Tanzania, Burundi, France, Canada, and the United States of America on 15 October 2007, twenty years after his assassination. The sorely-missed African legend that got eliminated from the geopolitical arena by the neocolonial forces of this world and their African puppets and compradors, just as he was beginning to stir the dream of Pan-Africanism again, was exhumed in 2015 following a request by his family.

The exhumation took place one year after the popular uprising that forced Blaise Compare out of power and compelled him to flee Burkina Faso into exile in neighboring Ivory Coast. Public anger against Blaise Compaore that had been building since the assassination of Sankara in 1987 spilled over into the streets after Compaore's 2014 attempt to change the constitution that would have allowed him to run for office again for the fifth time and for two more terms in what is generally considered election masquerades — a trend seen in authoritarian and hybrid regimes, especially in Francophone Africa in which the elections that are conducted are predetermined, though the stakeholders fake the whole process as democratic, thereby disguising the authoritarianism of their political systems under a thin veil of electoral legitimacy. The game plan also involves their puppet masters—the big powers, usually western—giving their approval to the masquerade with messages of congratulation to the incumbents or their chosen successors, thereby effectively recognizing the results of the election, and sustaining the comprador and system in place against the interest of people and the country. Compaore was trying to emulate Paul Biya of Cameroon (in power since 1982), who changed the constitution of the country again in 2008 to allow him two seven-year terms in office, and then used his security forces to crush the Cameroonians who came out to the streets to show their disapproval, killing 150 protesters in the process, but he was not as astute as his Cameroonian counterpart who was even more unpopular but managed to pull off the gamble.

An autopsy report which was conducted on the exhumed remains of Thomas Sankara revealed that the anti-imperialist revolutionary died from dozens of gunshot wounds, ruling out the feeble claim that his assassins killed him by mistake, as his onetime closest friend and successor tried to convince the world after his death. As Ambroise Farama, one of the lawyers representing the Sankara family said, it was *"...mind-boggling...You could say he was purely and simply riddled with bullets,"* On the contrary, the autopsies on the bodies of the other 12 soldiers killed and buried with Sankara in 1987 revealed that they had suffered only one or two gunshot wounds.

Burkina Faso restored Thomas Sankara's legacy as a revolutionary, a pan-Africanist, an environmentalist, a feminist, and a humanitarian with a bronze statue in the capital city of Ouagadougou in March 2019. However, the statue would be corrected a year later in May 2020, making it more imposing and truer to life than the previous one.

A statue of Thomas Sankara in May 2020

Three decades after the assassination of Thomas Sankara, the youths of Africa who are trying to find their bearings, still reserve a high place for the African revolutionary icon as one of those rare contemporary figures which the continent has produced that can be hailed as a model and a figure to identify with. His legacy is fast expanding beyond Africa as more and more people recognize him as a precursor of environmental struggle, as an outstanding figure in the case against financial globalism, as an advocate for the non-payment of illegitimate debts, and as a prototype of self-reliant development against the liberal model of development that benefits only a small minority.

As a matter of fact, today, numerous books, articles

and other works of art glorify the selfless African legend who took upon himself the colossal task of putting the people on their feet and showing them the path to a future devoid of neocolonialist influence that is wrapped up in trade, finance and imported cultures that undermine the strength of African communalist values and the sacredness of the family.

Democracy Index: Africa and the World

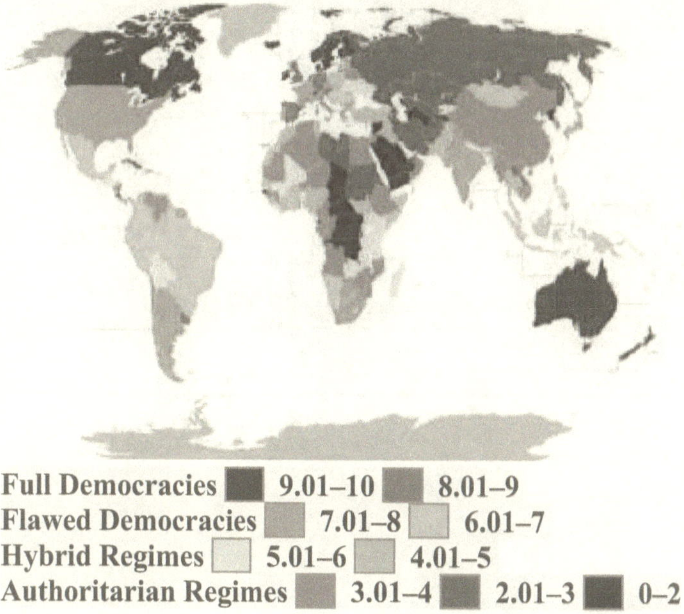

African Countries